ANNE GEDDES ™

Down in the Garden

ALPHABET
BOOK

Cedco

ISBN 0-7683-2005-4

© Anne Geddes 1997

Published in 1997 by Cedco Publishing Company,
2955 Kerner Blvd, San Rafael, CA 94901

First USA edition, July 1997

Designed by Denise Elliott
Produced by Kel Geddes
Color separations by Image Centre

Printed through South China Printing Co. Ltd, Hong Kong

Please write to us for a FREE FULL COLOR catalog of our fine Anne Geddes
calendars and books, Cedco Publishing Company, 2955 Kerner Blvd.,
San Rafael, CA 94901.

Anne Geddes is an Australian born professional photographer living in Auckland, New Zealand.

The worldwide success of her best selling book *Down in the Garden* continues to reinforce the title that Anne has earned of being the pre-eminent photographer of children in the world today.

Anne has said the following about her work, "I am frequently asked why I photograph babies so often, and where my ideas come from. Little babies are indeed my inspiration, and I cannot imagine a photographic life without them playing a major part in it. Where this special love for babies comes from I cannot tell you, and I have spent much time searching for an answer myself. All I know is that they are all perfect little human beings in their own ways, and we should all take the time to cherish them, especially while they are very small."

We know that you will enjoy sharing time with your children as you experience with them the unique and enchanting images contained in this *Down in the Garden Alphabet Book*.

A

ACORNS

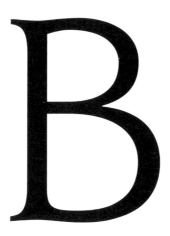

monarch

BUTTERFLY

C

three

spring

CARROTS

D

DAFFODILS

baby
CHICK
with

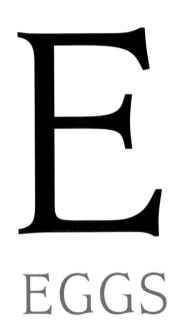

EGGS

F

FAIRY

G

GNOME

fishing

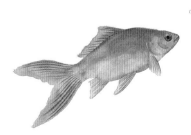

H

sleeping

HEDGEHOGS

I

INSIDE

J

JUG

of
f l o w e r s

K

sleeping

KITTEN

L

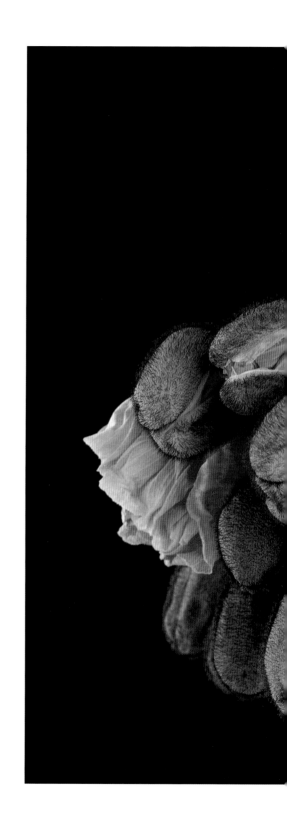

LADYBUGS

M

field

MICE

RED ROBIN

in

NEST

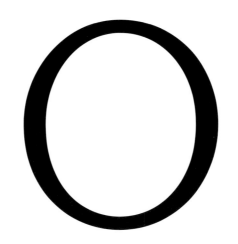

three

ORANGE

pots

P

PEAS

in

PODS

Q
QUIET
tiny
FAIRY
asleep

R

ROSE

S

Julia

SNAIL

T

the
TEDDYBEARS
picnic

U

flower

URN

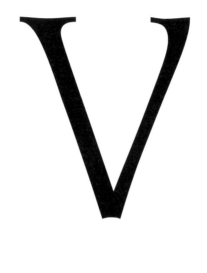

VASE

of

ROSES

W

WATERLILY

X

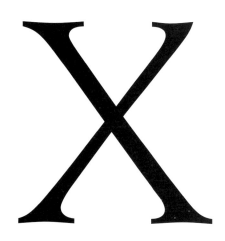

one

eXTRA

Y

YELLOW

daffodils

Z

Z
Z
Z
Z
Z
Z